A Friend like ZEEK

By Serena Arvayo

Illustrated by Bijan Samaddar

A friend like Zeek

Illustrated by Bijan Samaddar

www.aFriendlikeZeek.com

Contact: Info@afriendlikezeek.com

To Zeek

Love always,

Mama

This book belongs to:

_____

It's a sunny day in March and Zoey wants to visit her favorite park. Zoey is a very curious, silly, and outgoing girl who has many friends at school.

Zoey will make a very special friend today, different from all her other friends. His name is Zeek and she will never forget the day they met.

"I want this swing!" Zoey shouts as she runs as fast as she can to the last open swing. Zoey notices the older boy next to her, in a much bigger swing. Zoey isn't too shy to ask questions, even if she doesn't know the boy next to her.

"Hi! I'm Zoey! Do you want to play with me?" she asks Zeek cheerfully. He stares at her with a big smile and flaps his hands, making grunting sounds. "AHHHHH!"

Zoey notices Zeek is holding an iPad with picture icons in one hand, and a sock in the other.

"Hello? Do you want to play with me? Why are you holding a sock? Why did you bring your iPad to the park? How old are you?" asks Zoey.

Zeek continues to smile at Zoey and starts to laugh nervously, He covers both of his ears with his hands. "His name is Zeek," Zeek's mom says.

"Why isn't he talking to me?" asks Zoey, frowning.

"Zeek is smiling at you. He wants to play and wants to talk to you, but in his own way. Zeek has Autism. He is non-verbal. He uses his iPad to help him communicate without speaking with words like you and me. This is called an AAC device."

"Aw-tiz-um?" Zoey asks, looking confused. "I don't know anything about that!"

Zeek's mom smiles. "It's good to ask questions. The more you learn about kids who are different, the better you can understand them and have a friend like Zeek."

Zoey smiles and moves closer to Zeek.

"So... why does he have a sock? Can I see how he talks?"

Zeek's mom stops pushing him. He starts to grunt and make loud sounds Zoey has never heard before. Zeek gets upset. He flaps his sock around and plays with it anxiously. "You see, Zeek cannot say that he wants me to keep pushing him, so he gets frustrated easily. Wouldn't you feel frustrated if you couldn't say how you feel when you are sad or upset?"

Zoey looks at Zeek with a worried face. "Yes, I would be frustrated all the time!" Zoey exclaims. "Zeek flaps his sock to help him feel calm. It is called "stimming". It helps him feel better when he is frustrated."

Zeek puts his hands together and signs for 'more'.

"What did that mean, What is he doing with his hands?" asks Zoey.

"That's sign language. Zeek just made the sign for 'more', which means he wants me to push him more on the swing. Many people use sign language instead of words to communicate. You can learn it too!"

Zeek suddenly gets off the swing and takes Zoey's hand. He guides her to the playground. "What does he want?" asks Zoey.

"He wants to play with you and wants to show you where he wants to go!" his mom says.

Zeek takes Zoey to the slide to watch her go down. "Oh, okay, Zeek! Let's go down the slide together!" Zoey says.

A group of boys from across the playground run by Zeek and Zoey. "Did you hear those weird sounds? Why is that kid making those noises and holding a sock? That's WEIRD!" They all start to laugh.

Zeek covers his ears with his hands. Their loud voices make him uncomfortable. Now that Zoey has learned so much about Zeek, this makes her upset.

Zoey stomps over to the group of boys. "Hey! Listen! That boy has a name and it is Zeek! He is different and that's okay, he has Autism. He makes those sounds because he has a different way of talking. He still has feelings and he's my friend. Don't be mean!" The group of boys get quiet and feel ashamed.

Zeek's mom's eyes fill with tears of joy and pride. "Thank you for standing up for Zeek, Zoey," she says. "It's important that everyone respects people who are different than them. Everyone has feelings and deserves to be treated with care and kindness. Zeek can understand and his feelings are important."

We are all different in some way. We have different eyes, hair, skin, likes and dislikes. What makes us different makes us unique and beautiful.

Imagine a world where we all looked the same and had the same personalities? How boring would that world be? Being different and having Autism, or any other type of disabilities, does not mean that person doesn't deserve the same love and kindness as you and I.

Imagine if your little brother or sister had Autism like Zeek. You would want them to feel loved and protected, right? What about your best friend? You want to love and protect your friends and it would make you sad if someone was mean or said ugly words to them.

Treat everyone with Autism and other disabilities like your brother, sister or friend. Be kind to them, ask them if you can help, stand up to a bully for them, or try and learn more if you don't understand. We're all in this world to love and be kind to each other!

Thank you for reading!

Please share this book with all of your friends and family! This book is dedicated to my son Ezekiel and all his friends and family living with Autism: Ryker, Danny, Aubrey, Jaiden, Santiago, Alejandro, Mia, Analisa, Sami, and all those who live with Autism and other disabilities around the world.

To Zeek,

this journey we navigate together has been a rollercoaster ride and beautiful struggle the past 10 years. Thank you for teaching me true strength. I will forever advocate for you to be seen, understood, and accepted. I hope this book brings awareness and encourages people to learn more, be kinder, and teach their children about Autism and all the others just like you.

About the Author

My name is Serena Arvayo and I'm Zeek's mom. I have learned a lot over the past 10 years with Zeek and I was inspired to write this book to educate

children and people about non-verbal communication and moderate to severe Autism. Zeek was diagnosed at 2 years old and I was a very young mom at the time, trying to balance life with Zeek and beginning my career in healthcare. I always felt in my heart I wanted to do more to inspire, stay positive, and do something important as an Autism mom. I was inspired by a day we went to the park and a little girl asked so many questions about Zeek. I was touched by her genuine curiosity to want to know him. Going to the park and public places can sometimes cause major anxiety for both myself and for Zeek.

Sometimes being around a lot of people and being stared at makes day to day life uncomfortable. I was inspired by these situations to write a children's book as a fun way to educate kids about Autism. My dream for Zeek and all those living with Autism and other disabilities is a more inclusive world. A world where smiles are offered more than staring and more children and people are educated on the spectrum of Autism.

We are blessed with a very supportive family and friends in our lives that love and support us unconditionally, thank you all.

Support special needs🖤
small business owners!

Our friends:

'Jai at Play': Jaiden & Shekira

A Mother-Son Duo both diagnosed ASD- start business to raise positive Autism Awareness & Representation, Check out their Ausome flashcards!

jai-at-play.myshopify.com
Social media: @Jai_at_play

Amorcita:

Clothing Brand owned by special needs mama of beautiful little girl with Down Syndrome (Amorcita).
Stylish parent/family advocating clothing and more:
www.amorcitaclothing.com

Sensor E Play- Sensory Play Toys
by fellow Autism Mama
@sensoreplay

The End

Made in the USA
Las Vegas, NV
11 June 2022